WE ARE ALL APES

We Are All Apes
First hardcover edition: October 2021

Text © Aron Ra, 2021
Illustrations © Elisa Ancori, 2021
© 2021 Thule Ediciones, SL
Alcalá de Guadaíra 26, bajos. 08020 Barcelona
www.thuleediciones.com

Director of collection: José Díaz
Design & layout: Jennifer Carná
Contributor: SJ Beck
Scientific advisor: José Ramón Alonso

To request permissions, contact the publisher at info@thuleediciones.com

ISBN: 978-84-18702-12-9
D. L.: B 14829-2021

Printed in Spain by Índice Arts Gràfiques

WE ARE ALL APES

Aron Ra

Illustrations by Elisa Ancori

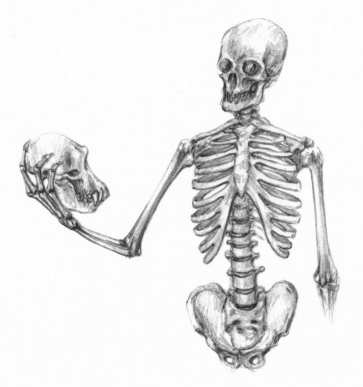

Contributor: SJ Beck

Scientific Advisor: José Ramón Alonso

thule

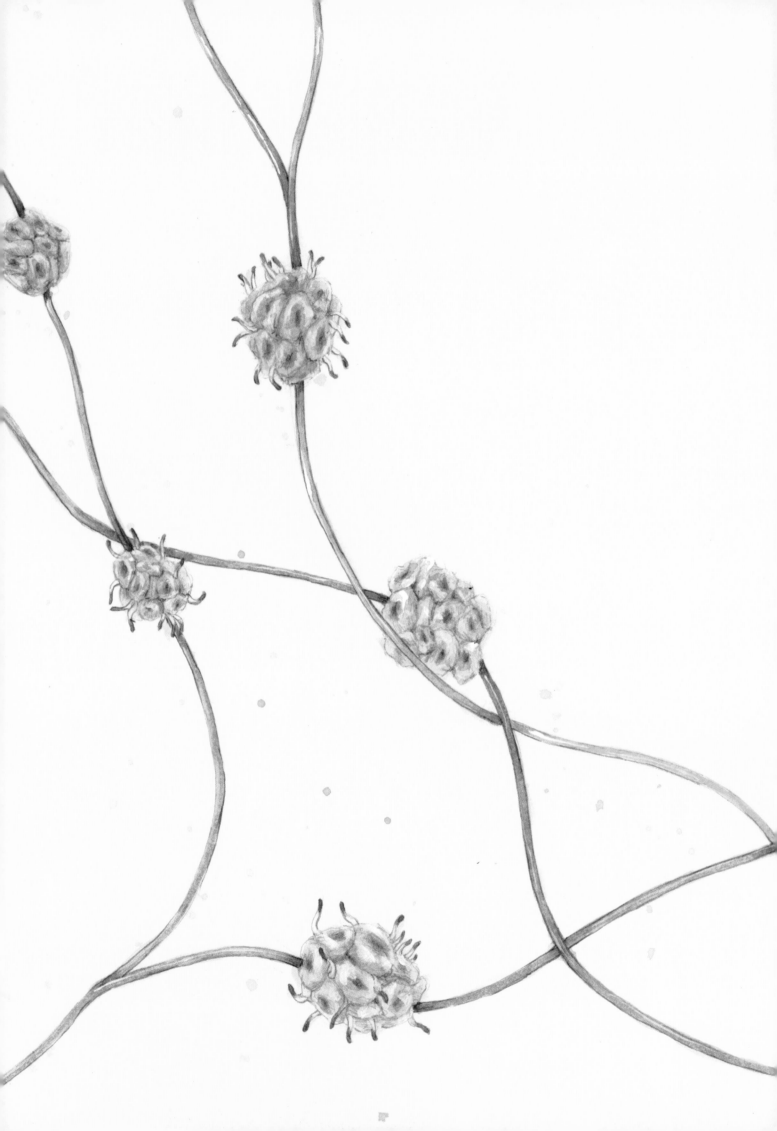

YOU ARE A METABOLIC ORGANISM

As such, you are basically a collection of replicative proteins that function according to chemical reactions and processes organized in cells. Your body digests food, converts it to energy, lipids, nucleic acids and proteins for your cells, and eliminates wastes. All of your cells work together, like a factory, to form the final living, breathing organism — you.

A virus is similar, in that it too has protein with mutable nucleic acids, just as you have. But viruses lack metabolism, and so may not be considered to be alive in the same manner that you definitely are as, to reproduce, they need to hijack cellular machinery from living hosts, like yourself.

YOU ARE AN EUKARYOTE

All organic life is distinguished by structural
differences at the cellular level between
different groups of prokaryotes (which are
essentially bacteria) and the eukaryotes (us).
Unlike bacteria or viruses, our cells have
the DNA enclosed in a nucleus with a few
exceptions like mature blood cells, which split
themselves away from their nucleus, so more
space becomes available to carry oxygen.
Likewise, your hair, nails, outer layer of skin
cells replace their nucleus with keratin as they
mature to toughen up. You can cut your nails
and hair because those cells are dead. Hence,
neither viruses nor prokaryote lifeforms are as
we are; eukaryotes.

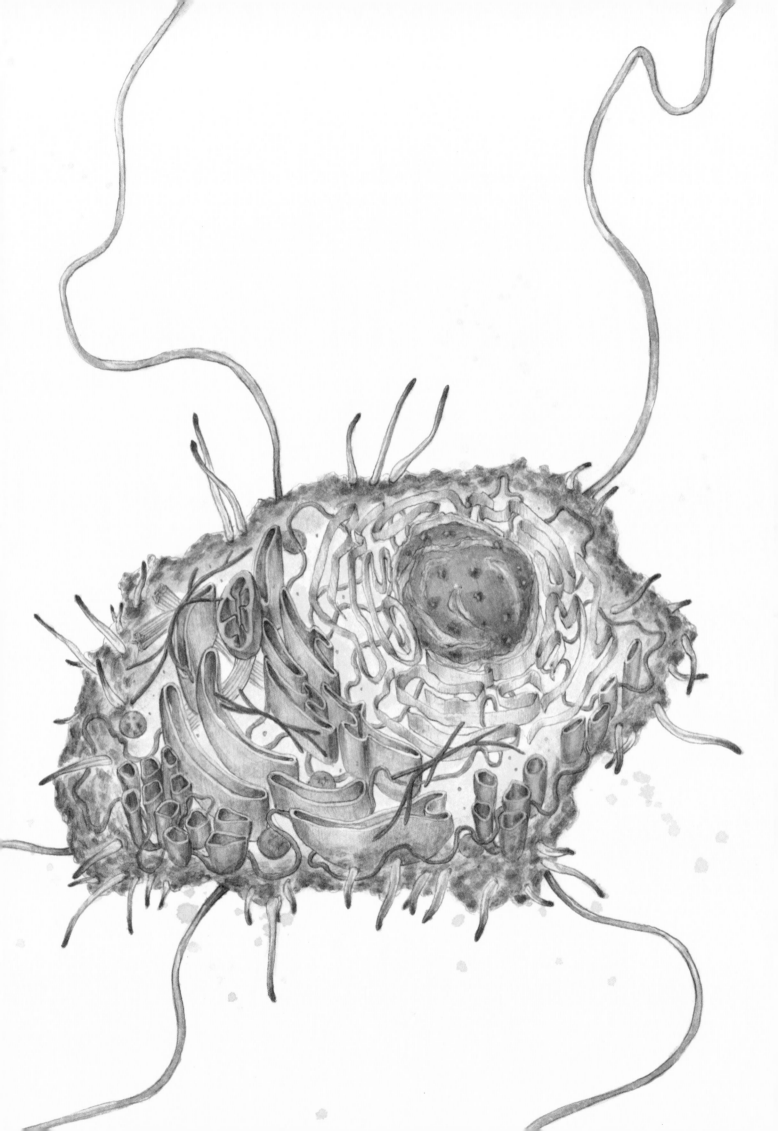

YOU ARE AN ANIMAL

Now I've heard a few creationists argue that there are plants and there are animals and then there are human beings. And that none of them are actually related to one another other than through a common creator. They adamantly argue that we are not animals, as if there is some insult in that association. But you are one of a few taxonomic kingdoms of eukaryotic life forms, *Animalia*.

Unlike those of most other biological kingdoms, like the plant kingdom, you are incapable of manufacturing your own food and must compensate for that by ingesting other organisms. In other words, your most basic structure requires that you cause death to other living things. Otherwise, you wouldn't have a means of digestion. This, along with some very specific anatomical differences in the chemical composition and organization of our metazoic cells. For instance, plants have chloroplasts to convert the sun's energy and you don't. Even their waste elimination isn't as gross. Instead of pooping, a tree moves waste to its outer layers. Therefore, the pages of this book contain plant waste. However, as an animal, you get to move on your own to search for food. It isn't always easy to be green.

These are the factors that define and distinguish an animal like yourself from all other kingdoms of life. Given the alternative choices between plants, molds, unicellular protists, or fungus, Animalia should seem reasonable even to the most adamant fundamentalist.

YOU ARE A CHORDATE

You have a spinal chord, a notochord, and every other minute physical distinction of that classification. You also have a skull, which classifies you as a craniate. Note: Not all chordates have skulls, or even bones of any kind. Once one of the chordates has enough calcium deposited around the brain to count as a skull, all of its descendants will share that. This is why absolutely all animals with skulls — like you — have a spinal cord that connects the rest of their body to the brain. And that is yet another commonality that implies common ancestry as opposed to common design.

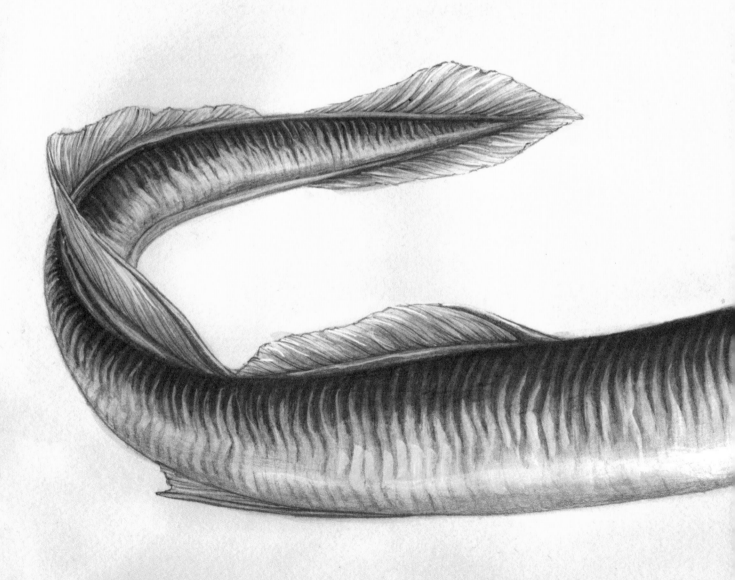

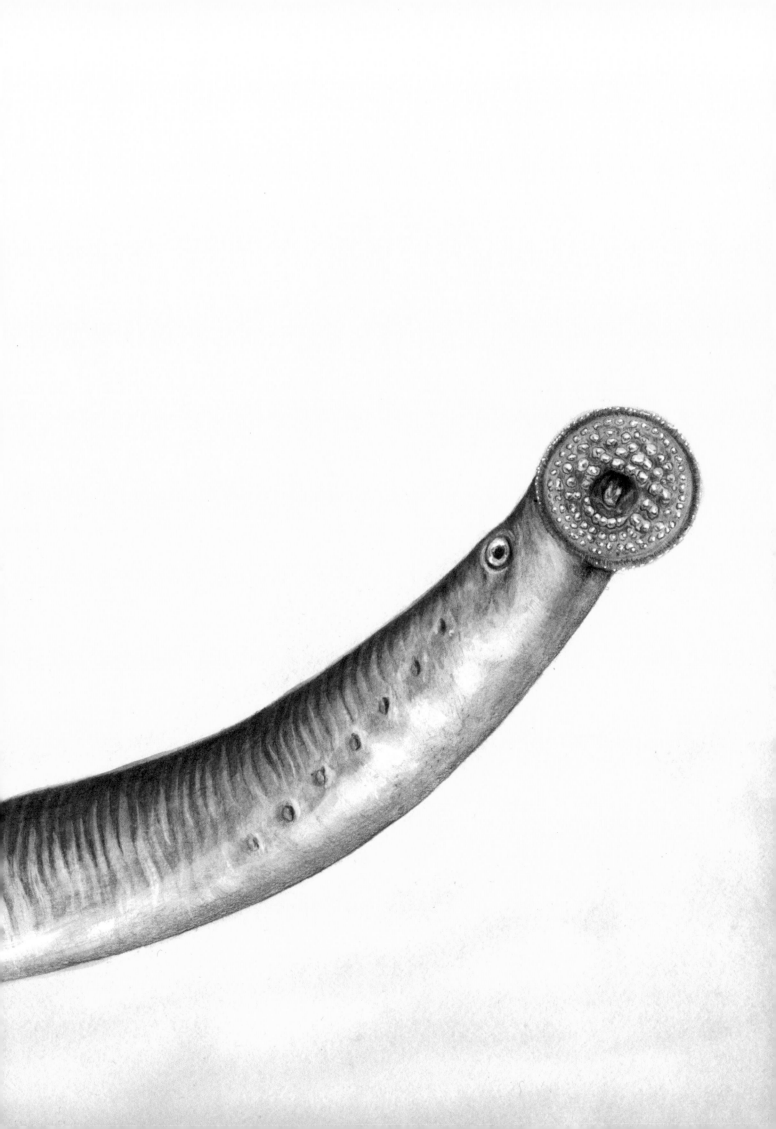

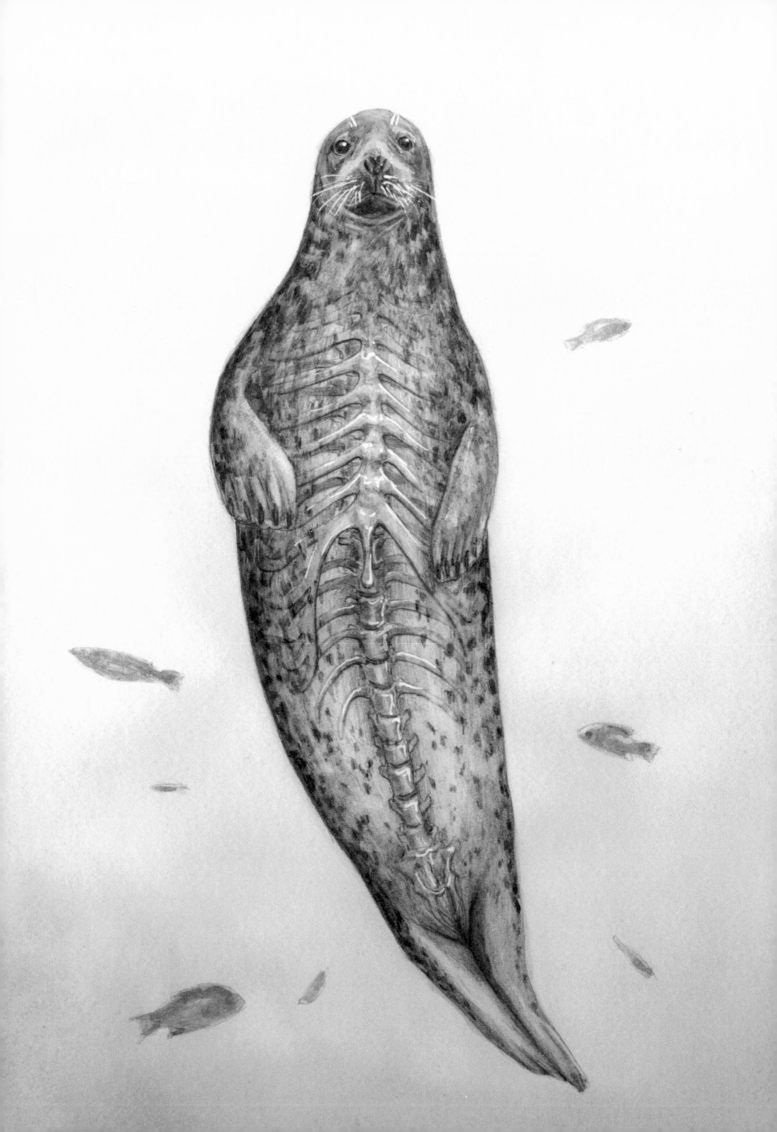

YOU ARE A VERTEBRATE

Like all mammals, birds, reptiles (dinosaurs included), amphibians, and most fish, you have a spine. Not everything with a spinal cord has a spine to put it in, but everything with a spine has a spinal cord in it, implying common descent. Every animal that has a jaw and teeth (*Gnathostomata*) also has a backbone. And of course, you have both as well, again implying common evolutionary history.

YOU ARE A TETRAPOD

You have only four limbs. So you are like all other terrestrial vertebrates including frogs. Even snakes and whales are tetrapods in that both still retain vestigial or fetal evidence of all four limbs. This is yet another consistent commonality implying a genetic relationship. There certainly is no creationist explanation for it.

YOU ARE A SYNAPSID

Unlike reptiles, dinosaurs included, and birds (which are all diapsids), your skull has only one temporal fenestra, a hole behind each eye. In humans, it is filled in, but we can still see the outline of it where the temporalis muscle connects the jaw to the skull. This is a commonality between all of the vast collection of "mammal-like reptiles", which are now all extinct without any Biblical recognition or scriptural explanation either for their departure or their presence in the first place.

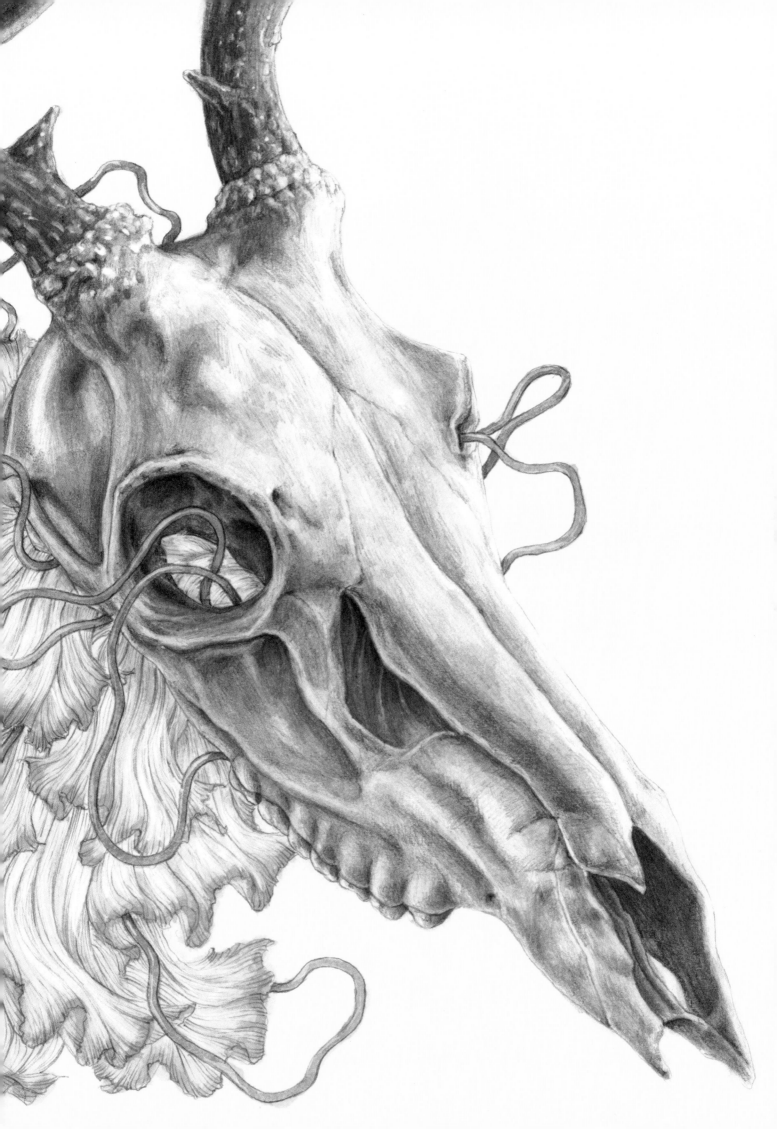

YOU ARE A MAMMAL

You are homeothermic (warm-blooded), follicle-bearing and have lactal nipples. The trade off for a warm-blooded metabolism is you have to eat more than a cold-blooded one, like a mature snake eats maybe once a week. And of course, not all synapsids are or were mammals, but all mammals are synapsid, implying common descent.

YOU ARE AN EUTHERIAN

Or more specifically, you are a placental mammal, like most other lactal animals from shrews to whales. All eutherians are mammals, but not all mammals are eutherian. There are a few major divisions in mammalia, only three of which still exist; those that hatch out of eggs like platypuses (monotremes), marsupials, that are born in the fetal stage and complete their development inside the mother's pouch, and those that developed in a shell-like placenta and were born in the infant stage, as you were.

Your own fetal development seems to reveal a similar track of development from a single cell to a tadpole-looking creature, then growing limbs and digits out of your fin-like appendages, and finally outgrowing your own tail. Some would consider this an indication of ancestry. Especially since fetal glass snakes, for example, actually have legs, feet, and cute little toes, which are reabsorbed into the body before hatching, implying common descent. Some fossil snakes also still had tiny back useless remnants of legs. The same is true of both fossil and fetal whales.

YOU ARE A PRIMATE

You have five fully-developed fingers and five fully-developed toes. Your toes are still prehensile and your hands can grasp with dexterity. You have only two lactal nipples and they are on your chest as opposed to your abdomen. These are pointless in males, which also have a pendulous penis and a well-developed ceacum or appendix, unlike all other mammals. Although your fangs are reduced in size, you do still have them along with some varied dentition indicative of primates exclusively. Your fur is thin and relatively sparse over most of your body. And your claws have been reduced to flat keratinized fingernails. Your fingers themselves have distinctive print patterns. As genetic diseases and disorders run in families, likewise, these genetic abnormalities also run in your evolutionary cousins in the primate order.

You are also susceptible to AIDS and are mortally allergic to the toxin of the male funnel web spider of Australia (which is especially deadly to all primates, which is why you'd better beware of these spiders). Unlike most other mammals, primates like us cannot produce vitamin-C naturally and must have it supplemented in our diet, just as all other primates do. Nearly every one of these individual traits are unique only to primates exclusively.

There is almost no other organism on Earth that matches any one of these descriptions separately, but absolutely all of the lemurs, tarsiers, monkeys, apes, you, and I match all of them at once perfectly, implying common descent.

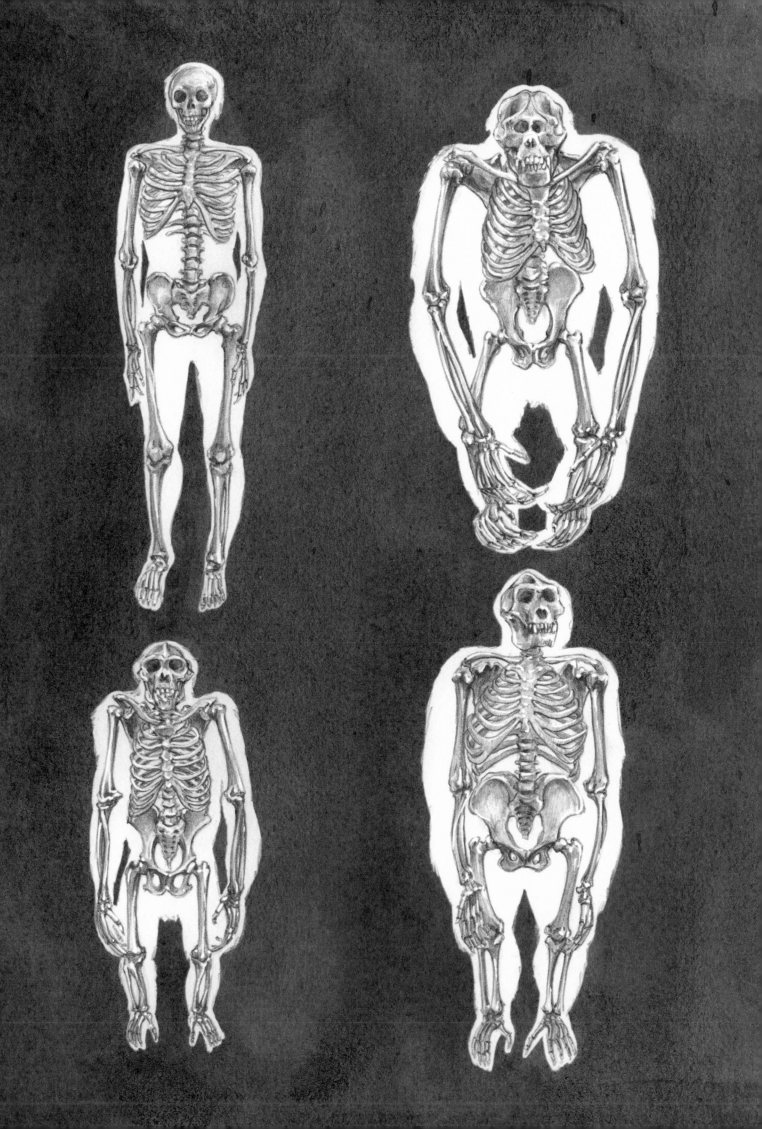

WE ARE ALL APES

Your tail is merely a stub of bones that don't
even protrude outside the skin. Your dentition
includes not only vestigial canines, but incisors,
cuspids, bicuspids, and distinctive molars that
come to five points interrupted by a "Y" shaped
crevasse. This, in addition to all of your other
traits, like the dramatically increased range of
motion in your shoulder, as well as a profound
increase in cranial capacity and disposition
toward a bipedal gait, indicates that you are
not merely a vertebrate cranial chordate and a
tetrapoidal placental mammalian primate, but
you are more specifically an ape, and so were
both of your parents before you.

Genetic similarity confirms morphological
similarity rather conclusively, just as Charles
Darwin himself predicted more than 150 years
ago. While he knew nothing of DNA of course,
he postulated that inheritable units of information
must be contributed by either parent. He rather
accurately predicted the discovery of DNA by
illustrating the need for it. Our 98.4% to 99.4%
identical genetic similarity explains why you have
such social, behavioral, sexual, developmental,
intellectual, and physical resemblance to a
chimpanzee. Similarities that are not shared with
any other organism on the planet. Hence you are
both different species of the same literal family.
In every respect, you are nearly identical.
We, my friend, are all apes.

ON THE UNDERGROUND

Set 1
On gratitude, love and madness

I Benediction

Text
AMES BERRY (b. 1924)

Mus
THEA MUS
(199

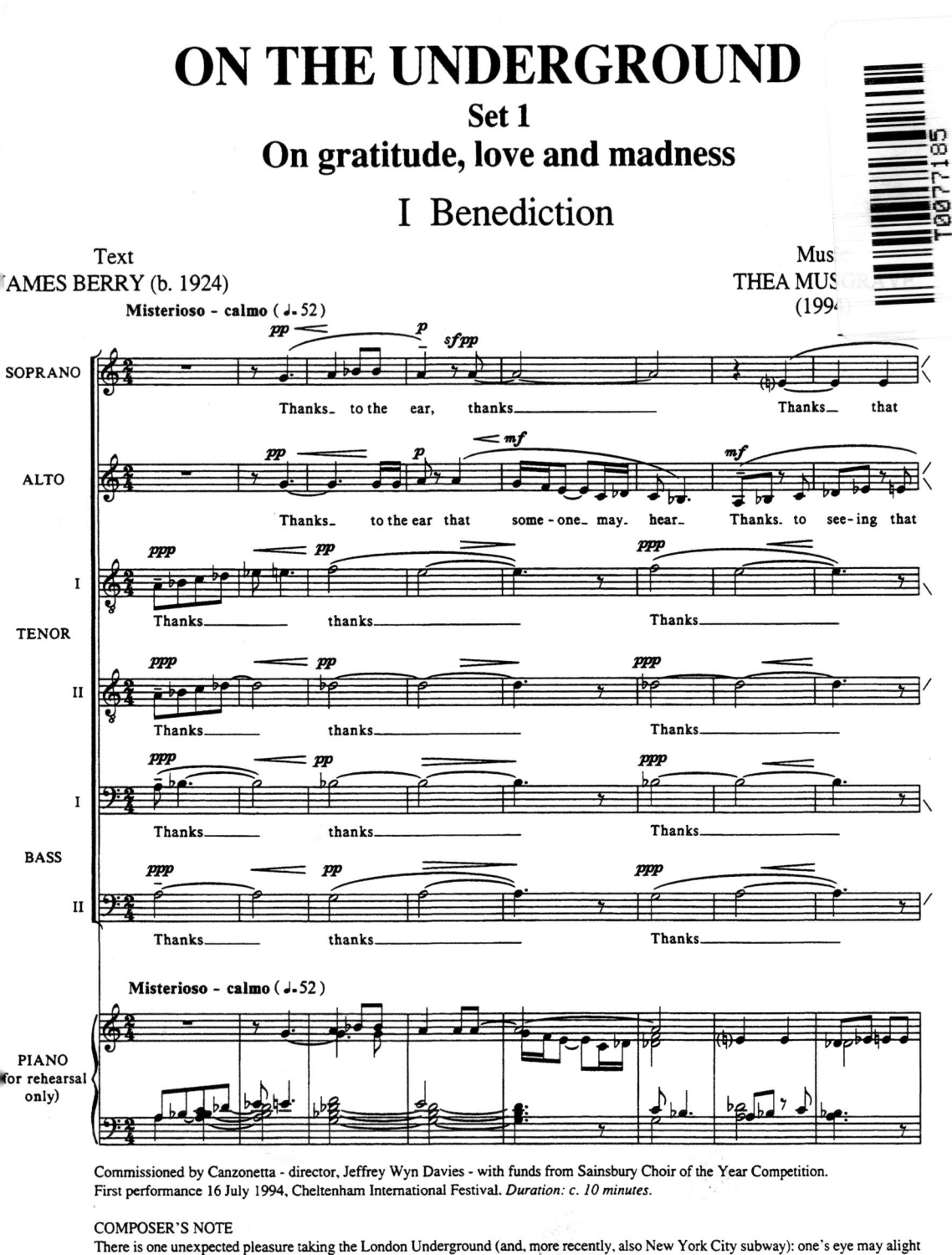

Commissioned by Canzonetta - director, Jeffrey Wyn Davies - with funds from Sainsbury Choir of the Year Competition.
First performance 16 July 1994, Cheltenham International Festival. *Duration: c. 10 minutes.*

COMPOSER'S NOTE

There is one unexpected pleasure taking the London Underground (and, more recently, also New York City subway): one's eye may alight on a poem placed amongst the pervasive numbing advertisements, and, for a moment, the imagination takes wing.

The six poems selected for this work are all to be found in *100 Poems on the Underground*. The first and last, *Benediction* by James Berry and *Sometimes* by Sheenagh Pugh are expressions of gratitude. The second poem *Her Anxiety* by Yeats, describes the inevitable death of true love. In the third poem Stevie Smith's Lady Singleton follows her own very eccentric ways, in contrast to Adrienne Rich's Aunt Jennifer of the fifth poem, who is trapped by the deadly weight of convention. In the third poem, *Much Madness is divinest Sense*, Emily Dickinson tells of how anybody flouting the majority opinion is "straightway dangerous and handled with a chain".

T.M

NOV 160270

24
SOP. I
SOP. II
ALTO I
ALTO II
TEN.
BASS
mf
dim.
p
pp
Thanks- to flow - er-ing of white moon
Thanks- to flow - er-ing of white moon
moon, to flow-er-ing of- white moon- and spread-ing- shawl- of- night
Thanks- to flow-er-ing of- white moon- and spread-ing- shawl- of- night
flow-er-ing of- white- moon- And spread - - ing shawl-
cres - - - cen - - do
And spread - - - - - - ing
31
mp
(mf)
div.
holding vil-lag-es and cit-ies to-ge-ther, to-ge-ther.
And spread-ing shawl- of black night Thanks.
of black night Thanks.
shawl of black night Thanks.
[circa 1'45"]

II Her Anxiety

Text
W.B. YEATS (1865-1939)

Music
THEA MUSGRAVE

10
mf
Such bo - dy lov - ers
p
Prove that I lie
mp
Prove_ that I lie_ that.
mf
div.
pp eco
Prove that I lie Prove that I lie.
Prove that I lie_ Prove that I lie.
div. mf
sfpp
Prove_ that_ I lie.
10
16
cres - - - - - cen - - - - - - - - do
f
have,_ such ex - act - - - ing breath_ that they touch or sigh_
mf
_ I lie. Lov - - ers_ touch_ Or_ they_ sigh_
unis.
p
Lov - ers touch_ Lov - - - - - - - - ers_ touch Or_ they
16

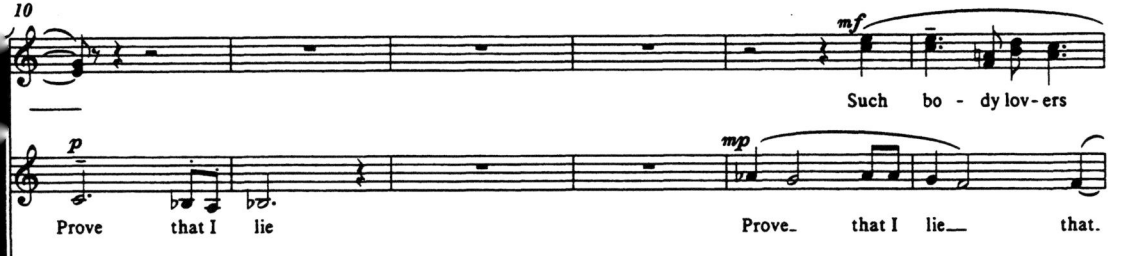

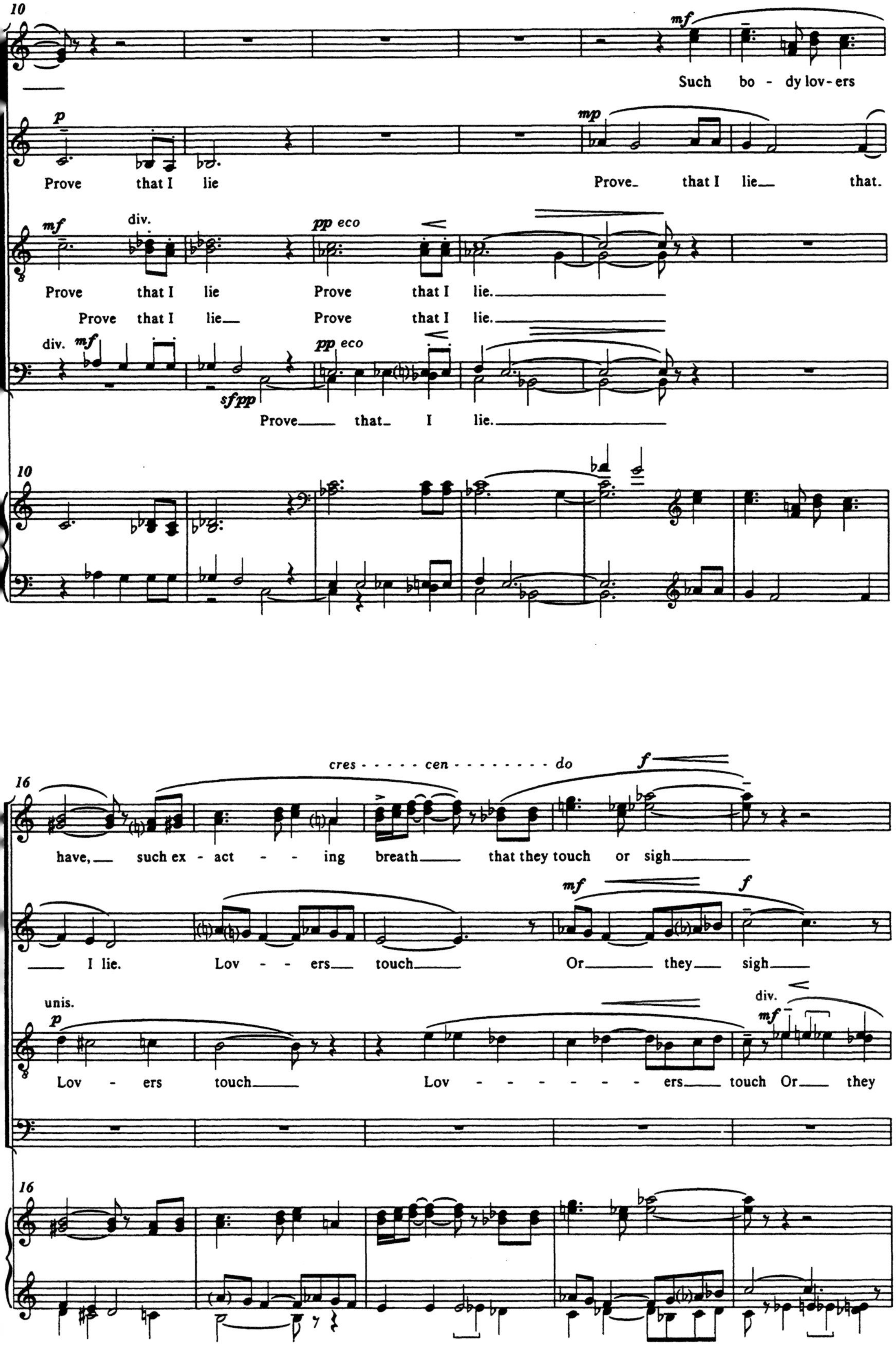

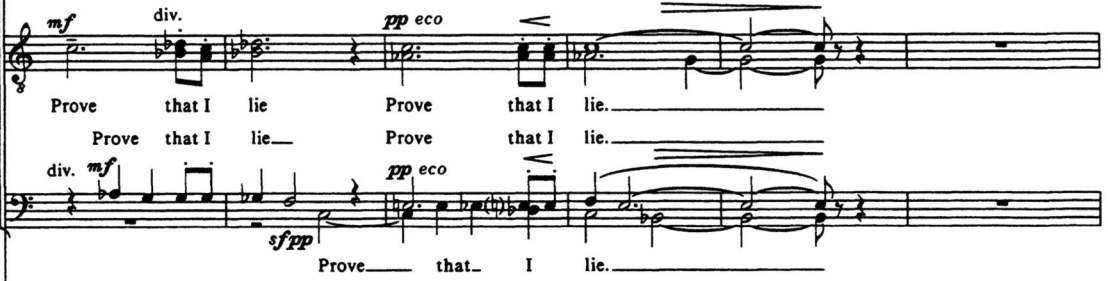

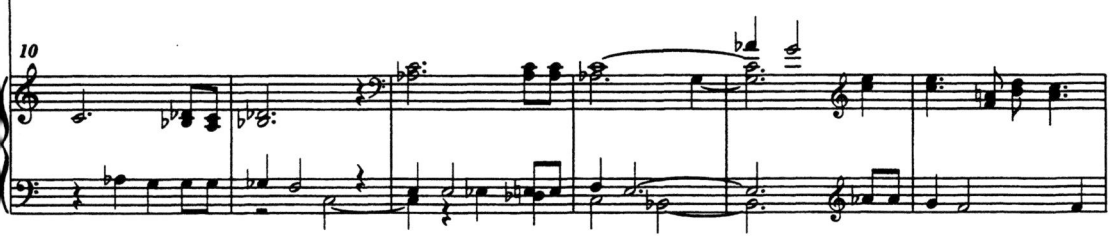

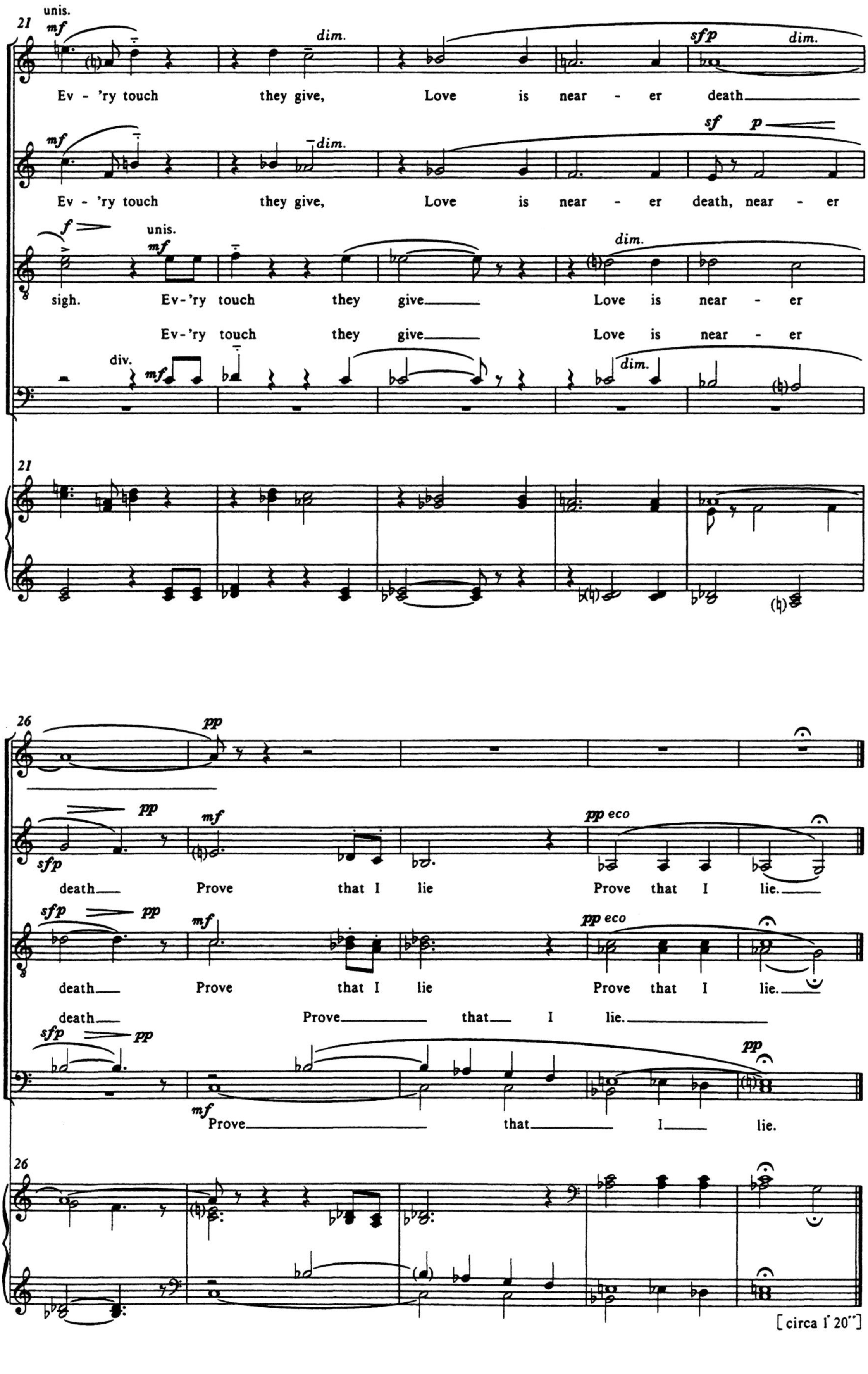
unis.
mf
dim.
sfp
Ev - 'ry touch they give, Love is near - er death
sf p
Ev - 'ry touch they give, Love is near - er death, near - er
f
sigh. Ev-'ry touch they give Love is near - er
Ev-'ry touch they give Love is near - er
div.
pp
death Prove that I lie Prove that I lie.
pp eco
death Prove that I lie Prove that I lie.
death Prove that I lie.
Prove that I lie.
[circa 1' 20'']

III Lady "Rogue" Singleton

Text
STEVIE SMITH (1902-1971)

Music
THEA MUSGRAVE

36
unis.
div.
mf
quasi gliss.
p
la
la la la la la la
you what' I feel for the e-le-phants and themi-as-mas and
la la la la la la la la la la la la
gliss.
la la la la
36

43
la la la
unis.
mf
la la la la la la la la la la la la la
p
the gen - - e-ral view la la la la la
div.
mf unis.
la la la la la la la la la Come, come La -
div.
unis.
la la la la la la la la la Come, come La -
43

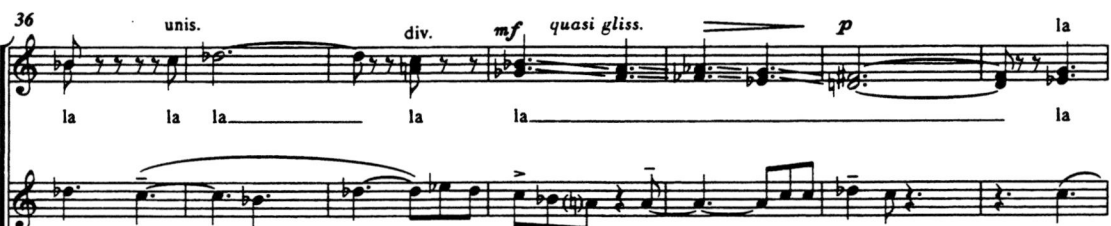

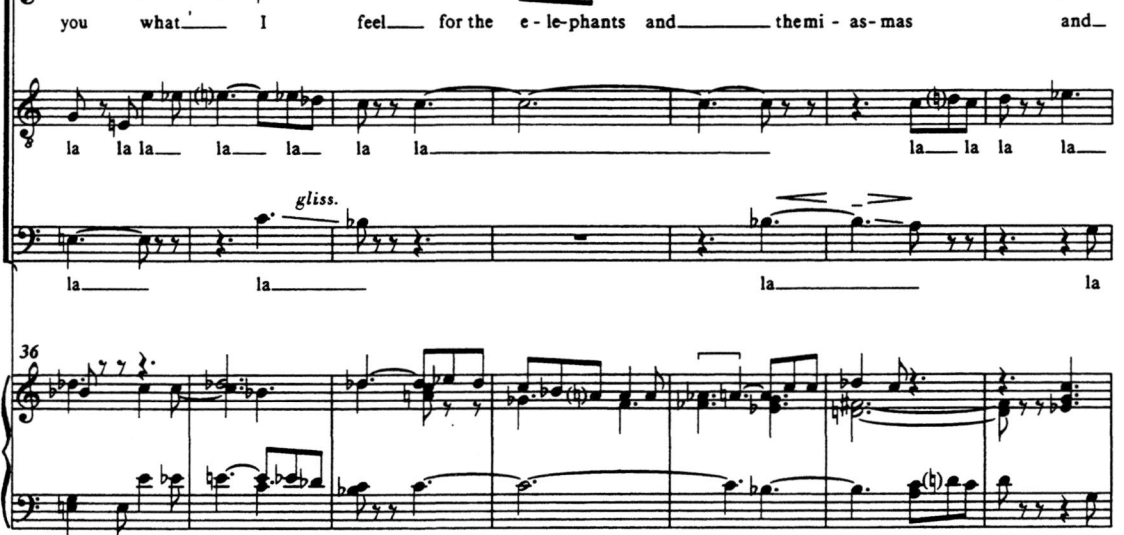

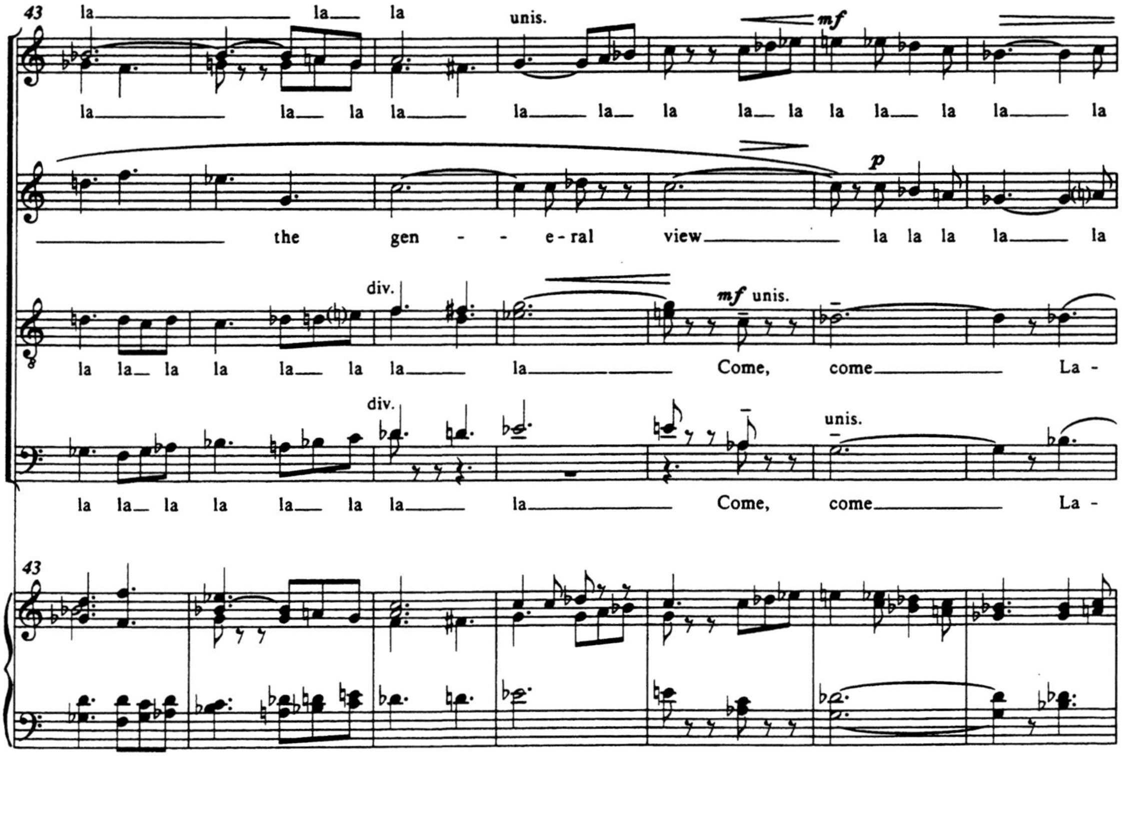

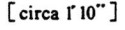
[circa 1' 10"]

IV Much Madness is divinest Sense

Text
EMILY DICKINSON (1830-86)

Music
THEA MUSGRAVE

*Stagger breathing and sustain 'A' steadily throughout!

© Copyright 1996 Novello & Company Limited

13

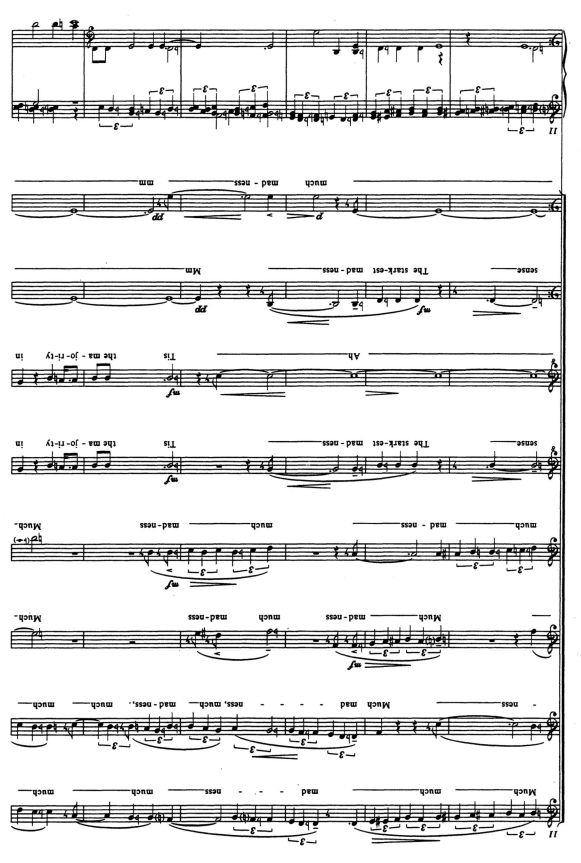

16

[circa 2']

V Aunt Jennifer's Tigers

Text
ADRIENNE RICH (b.1929)

Music
THEA MUSGRAVE

12
fear the men be-neath the tree They prance in
fear the men, the men be-neath the tree They prance,
cresc.
do not fear the men be-neath the tree They prance in
cresc.
do not fear the men be-neath the tree
mf
12

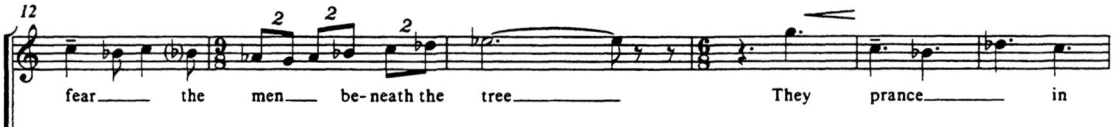

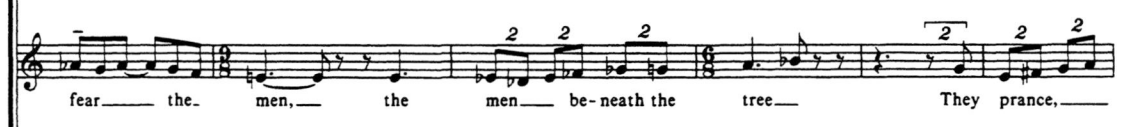

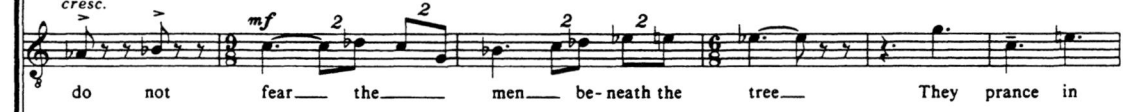

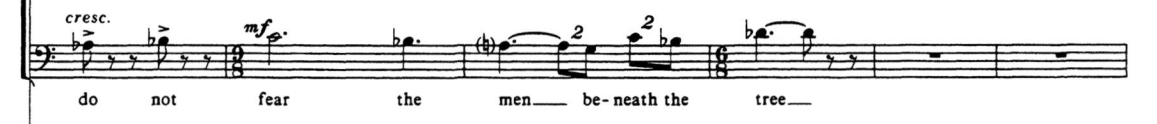

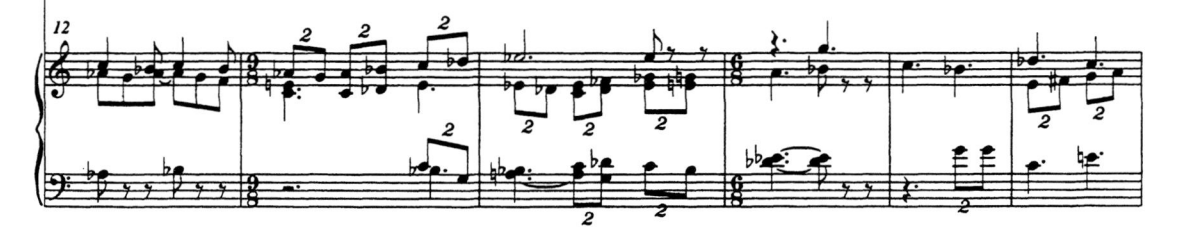

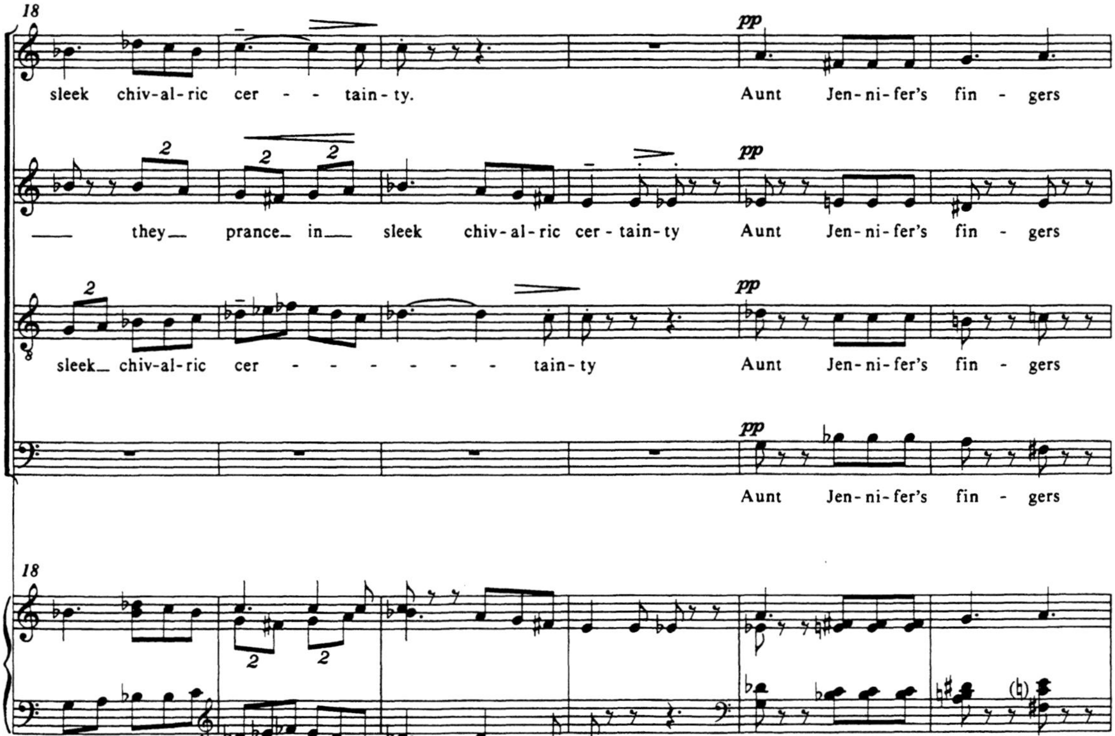
18
sleek chiv-al-ric cer - - tain-ty. Aunt Jen-ni-fer's fin - gers
they prance in sleek chiv-al-ric cer-tain-ty Aunt Jen-ni-fer's fin - gers
sleek chiv-al-ric cer - - - - - - - tain-ty Aunt Jen-ni-fer's fin - gers
Aunt Jen-ni-fer's fin - gers
pp
18

22

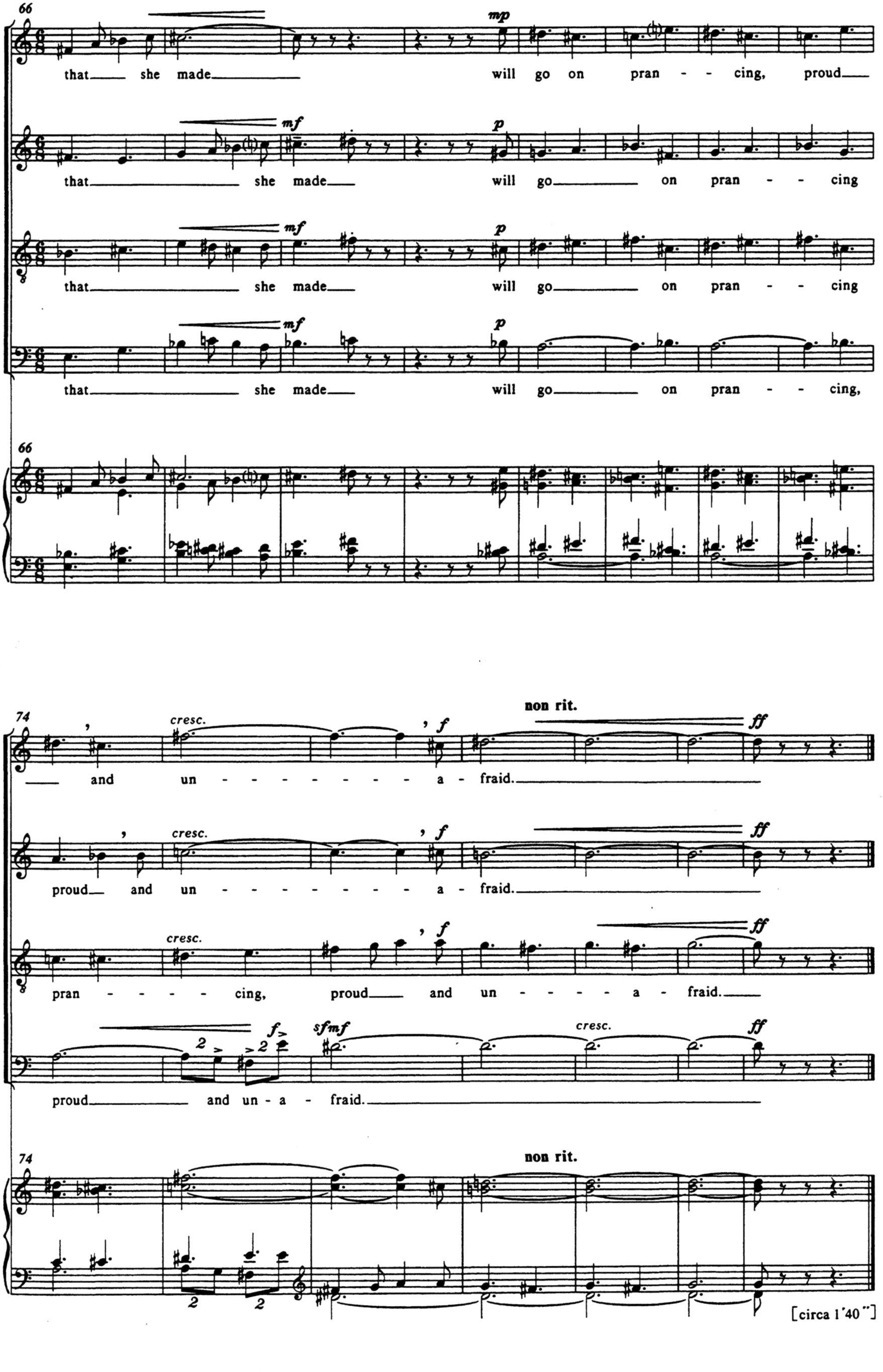

that__ she made_____ will go on pran - - cing, proud__

that_____ she made__ will go____ on pran - - cing

that_____ she made__ will go__ on pran - - cing

that____ she made__ will go___ on pran - - cing,

__ and un - - - - - - a - fraid._____

proud__ and un - - - - - - a - fraid._____

pran - - - - cing, proud__ and un - - - a - fraid.__

proud__ and un - a - fraid._____

[circa 1´40´´]

VI Sometimes

Text
SHEENAGH PUGH (b. 1950)

Music
THEA MUSGRAVE

28

[circa 2´]

d, Bury St Edmunds, Suffolk, IP33 3YB, UK

NOV160270